100 facts on Cats & Kittens

Steve Parker

Consultant: Camilla de la Bedoyere

Miles Kelly

PUBLISHING

First published in 2008 by Miles Kelly Publishing Ltd
Bardfield Centre, Great Bardfield, Essex, CM7 4SL

material is also available in hardback and flexiback

2 4 6 8 10 9 7 5 3 1

Editorial Director Belinda Gallagher
Art Director Jo Brewer
Assistant Editor Hannah Todd
Editorial Assistant Carly Blake
Volume Designer Sophie Pelham
Picture Researcher Laura Faulder
Reprographics Anthony Cambray, Stephan Davis,
Liberty Newton, Ian Paulyn
Production Manager Elizabeth Brunwin

ISBN 978-1-84236-968-5

Printed in China

British Library Cataloguing-in-Publication Data
A catalogue record for this book is available from the British Library

ACKNOWLEDGEMENTS
The publishers would like to thank the following artists
who have contributed to this book:
Ann Baum (Linda Rogers)/Martin Camm,/Mark Davis(Mackerel)/Mike Foster
Sauro Giampaia/Ian Jackson/Andrea Morandi/Julia Pewsey (Linden Artists)
Steve Roberts/Eric Rowe (Linden Artists)/Mike Saunders
Mike Taylor (Wildlife Art)/Mike White (Temple Rogers)
Cartoons by Mark Davis at Mackerel
Cover artwork by Ian Jackson
All other artworks come from Miles Kelly Archives
The publishers would like to thank the following sources for the use
of their photographs:
P15(BR) Jo Brewer; P26 Anthony Cambray; P42(T) Mark Henry, (B) pictorialpress.com;
P45(T) Sandra North; P47(B) Hanna-Barbera/pictorialpress.com

All other photographs from:
Castrol, CMCD, Corbis, Corel, digitalSTOCK, digitalvision, Flat Earth, Hemera, ILN,
John Foxx, PhotoAlto, PhotoDisc, PhotoEssentials, PhotoPro, Stockbyte

www.mileskelly.net
info@mileskelly.net

www.factsforprojects.com

Contents

Cats are cool

1 **Cats make great pets.** Perhaps your family has a cat? These creatures can be warm, friendly and funny. They are quite independent and don't need as much attention as dogs do. However, cats still need our care – fresh food and water every day, a safe place to sleep and someone to look after their health.

◀ A mother cat, or queen, relaxes with her kittens. The female cat is one of the animal world's best mothers. She watches over her kittens day and night, feeds them with her milk, and licks, cleans and grooms them.

Feline family

2 **All the cats in the world form one big family – what animal experts call the family Felidae.** This includes about 38 different kinds or species of cat, from massive tigers and lions to our own pet cats. The cat family belongs to the larger group of mammals called carnivores, along with dogs, foxes, wolves, stoats and weasels.

▼ The sabre–tooth cat *Smilodon* was bigger than a tiger and lived in North America. It died out about 10,000 years ago.

3 **Big cats include lions, tigers, leopards, snow leopards, clouded leopards, jaguars and cheetahs.** The biggest are tigers, especially the Siberian tiger that lives in cold, snowy northeast Asia. It can grow to 3 metres long including its tail, and weigh up to 350 kilograms. That's 100 times heavier than a pet cat!

◄ The tiger's dark stripes help it to hide in long grass and tangled undergrowth.

4 **The cheetah is the world's fastest runner, at 100 kilometres an hour.** In ancient times rich people raised cheetahs in North Africa and the Middle East. They were put on leads, like dogs. However, they were never truly tamed, and often escaped.

5 The large cat with the most names is the cougar – also called the mountain lion, puma or American panther. People tried to tame young cougars and keep them as pets. But as they grew, their wild instincts, or feelings, become stronger. A fully grown cougar can be very dangerous.

▲ Cougars live from the north of North America, all the way down to the south of South America.

6 There are about 20 kinds of medium-sized cats. Lynx live all around the north of the world and hunt hares and deer in cold forests and on icy mountains. In Africa the spotted serval preys on rats and birds. In Southeast Asia the fishing cat swims after frogs, crabs and fish.

▲ The serval has a slim body and long legs. It runs very fast, like its bigger cousin, the cheetah.

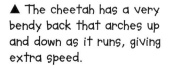

▲ The cheetah has a very bendy back that arches up and down as it runs, giving extra speed.

MAKE A SABRE-TOOTHED CAT MASK

You will need:
cardboard   paints   elastic   scissors
1. Ask an adult to cut out a cat's face shape from card.
2. Cut out holes for the eyes and paint on whiskers and fur.
3. Attach some elastic to go around the back of your head.
4. Put on your mask and growl!

Small cats in the wild

7 All kinds, or breeds, of pet cats belong to the same single type, or species, which scientists call *Felis cattus*. Some kinds of cats that live in the wild are even smaller than our pet cats. Most live in forests and jungles. Their fur is spotted and striped so that they blend in with the trees, branches and leaves, and their shadows. This means they can creep up on prey without being noticed.

8 The jungle cat of southern Asia is slightly larger than a pet cat. It is also called the reed or swamp cat since it hunts along the banks of rivers, swamps, pools and ditches. Its main food is rats, birds, lizards, snakes and fish. It also eats frogs and even toads. Unlike many cats, the jungle cat does not mind prowling about looking for food during the day. It often lives near villages and towns and does not seem to mind people nearby. However, it usually stays hidden among bushes and undergrowth.

▼ An adult jungle cat. Jungle cat kittens have close-set stripes and look like tiny tigers. However, the stripes fade as they grow up.

9 Nearly all cats are good climbers, but the margay of South America is one of the best climbers of all. It can run straight up a tree trunk – and run head-first straight down again! The margay is about the same size as a pet cat. Like all cats, it is a hunter. It catches squirrels, tree rats, possums and small birds.

▲ The Andean cat wraps its furry tail around itself when it sleeps, to keep warm in the bitter cold of the mountains.

▼ The black–footed cat has dark spots on its body that lengthen into rings on its legs and tail. It lives in hot, dry, rocky grasslands.

11 The Andean cat is small, only the size of a pet cat – but very tough. It lives high in the Andes Mountains of South America, like a tiny 'mountain lion'. Its thick fur protects it from the icy winds as it hunts small creatures.

10 The black–footed cat of southern Africa can weigh less than 2 kilograms. That's smaller than most pet cats, which usually weigh 3 to 4 kilograms. Because it is so little, the black-footed cat catches little prey too, such as small lizards, baby birds, spiders, and even worms and termites.

I DON'T BELIEVE IT!

Many cats were once hunted for their fur coats, which were used to make hats, boots, gloves and similar items. Today most cats in the wild are protected by law.

The first pets

12 All pet or domestic cats probably came from the cat species known as the wildcat (*Felis silvestris*). It looks like a slightly larger, heavier version of the pet cat known as the tabby. The wildcat still lives naturally in many places today, including Scotland, Europe, Africa and Asia. Sometimes wildcats breed with pet cats.

▶ A wildcat pauses to crouch on a branch, looking and listening for prey – or danger.

13 The first pet or domestic cats were tamed from the type of wildcat that lives in and around Egypt in north Africa. This is called the African or Abyssinian type of wildcat. It still survives today in the wild. If its kittens are taken in by people and reared from a very young age, they become friendly pets. In fact, this is how the first domestic cats gradually evolved. The European or forest type of wildcats, as found in Scotland, are much more 'wild' than their African cousin – they are fierce and almost impossible to tame, even if people raise them from tiny kittens.

◀ In ancient Egypt people worshipped a goddess called Bastet, who was kind and gentle. She looked after women and cats. Bastet sometimes appeared with the head of a lioness, when she was supposed to be protecting the king in battle.

14 We think the first domestic or pet cats date back to ancient Egypt, more than 5000 years ago. Perhaps this happened when African wildcats waited around houses or food and grain stores, attracted by pests such as mice and rats. The cats gradually got used to people, and the people became friendly with the helpful, pest-killing cats. When the Great Pyramids and temples of Egypt were built, important rulers or pharaohs were preserved as mummies – so were many cats.

15 There are pictures, statues and carvings of cats from ancient Greece and Rome, more than 2000 years ago. The Roman city of Pompeii was mostly destroyed when the volcano Mount Vesuvius erupted in the year AD79. A mosaic picture that was undamaged shows a tabby-like cat attacking a bird.

▲ The bodies of some Egyptian cats were preserved as mummies and buried in special tombs.

◀ The Abyssinian breed of pet cat is clever and friendly. It also likes freedom, so does not like being kept in a small place such as a town house.

16 Today the pet cat that is most like the very first domestic cats is probably the Abyssinian breed. It usually has large pointed ears, orange eyes, and brown or tawny fur with faint patches of darker brown or black.

Pet pampering

17 A cat can make a great pet – but only for certain people. A pet cat that receives care, comfort and companionship will be a loving friend for many years. However, some people simply don't like cats. They become nervous or worried when a cat is near. The cat senses this and becomes nervous too.

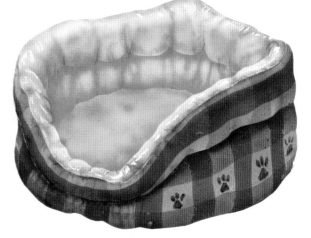

▲ A comfy cat basket is a safe place for warm naps.

◀ ▼ Small moving toys are fun to chase. A flea collar, comb and brush keep the cat's fur clean.

18 When people plan to get a pet cat, they should ask – 'Do we have time?' Like any pet, a cat needs regular food, water and comfort. Some people say that female cats are friendlier and less trouble, while males or toms are more independent and roam further. But every cat, like every human, has its own personality.

I DON'T BELIEVE IT!

Every year, thousands of cats are abandoned or made homeless by thoughtless owners. They are left to live as stray cats. This is why there are cat rescue centres.

19 It is a good idea to buy a basic 'cat kit' before your new pet arrives. This includes strong plastic bowls or dishes for food and drink, cat food, a brush, and usually a litter tray or box (toilet tray) for droppings. Some owners buy their cat lots of toys and a warm padded basket for sleeping. But part of the fun with cats is that they don't always do what we want, and they may ignore these luxuries!

20 There are many places to obtain a new pet cat, such as pet shops, friends, rescue centres, cat breeders and cat dealers. Generally, it's best to get a cat from someone who knows a lot about them and who can give proper advice. A new cat should be checked by a knowledgeable person such as a vet or local cat breeder.

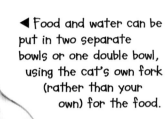

◀ Food and water can be put in two separate bowls or one double bowl, using the cat's own fork (rather than your own) for the food.

▶ A cat's lower body must be supported by one hand, so the cat feels safe and does not 'dangle'.

21 Cats are naturally clean animals. However we should always wash our hands after handling them, their food and their litter trays. Otherwise we could catch something from them – or they might catch something from us!

◀ A litter (toilet) tray must be checked every day, especially for cats that live mainly indoors.

22 Sometimes a cat does not want to be picked up, in which case it's best not to try – otherwise, you might get a scratch. If a cat does not mind, then it can be picked up carefully with both hands under the body, and held against our own body with the rear legs supported by our hand or arm. A cat must feel well supported and confident, or it will be frightened.

Mealtime

23 Cats are carnivores — their basic food is meat. This includes fish, and poultry such as chicken, as well as animal meat. Most pet foods made for cats contain much of the goodness they need. Dry cat biscuits are useful because they do not go rotten or bad as quickly as fresh meat if uneaten. Cats like to eat and drink without interference, so it's best not to stroke a cat when it is eating — just leave it alone.

24 It's best to give a cat different foods, so that it gets a wide range of nourishment. It's also best to feed a cat in the same place each time, preferably somewhere quiet and calm like a corner of a room, using its own clean feeding bowl and mat. Usually two meals each day are best — morning and evening. Kittens and young growing cats need to have smaller meals more often as they are using a lot of energy as they run around and grow.

▼ Two cats must get to know and trust each other before they will eat and drink close together. In the wild, they could be very hungry and try to steal each other's food.

25
Some owners give their cat treats such as specially cooked rich meats, cream and other titbits. This is fine now and again, but not every day. Cats may seem to be 'fussy eaters', always wanting the most expensive foods. But if they are hungry, they will soon eat cheaper foods.

26
Overweight cats can be unhealthy just like overweight people. Cats are naturally sleek hunters, and if they get too fat, they are at risk from various problems such as stiff joints and heart disease. It's unwise to give a cat too much food. Leftover meat soon goes smelly and rotten, and attracts pests such as flies. Adjust the amount you give so the cat's food bowl is virtually empty by the time of its next meal.

QUIZ
1. What are overweight cats particularly at risk of?
2. How often should you feed an adult cat?
3. Why is it a bad idea to leave leftover cat food lying around?

Answers:
1. Stiff joints and heart disease 2. Twice a day, once in the morning and once in the evening 3. It attracts pests such as flies

Supreme hunter

27 Everything about a cat is designed for silent, stealthy hunting – especially when it's dark. A pet cat is smaller than most other cat species, but is just the same in its body build and structure, or anatomy. It has strong muscles, padded paws for silent walking, excellent senses of sight and hearing, and sharp claws and teeth.

28 Inside its body, a cat has the same main parts as a dog, rabbit, horse, monkey and you – in fact, any mammal. It has a skeleton made of bones, a heart to pump blood, lungs to breathe air, and a stomach and intestines (guts) to digest food.

▲ A cat creeps towards its prey very slowly, bit by bit. It tries not to make any noise and crouches low to stay mostly hidden. If it feels the prey has noticed it, the cat may 'freeze' completely still, even for several minutes.

29

A cat has five clawed toes on each front paw, and four on each back paw. The innermost toe on the front paw is higher up on the side of the foot, more like a thumb. Usually, muscles pull the claws up and into the toe, hiding them in small pockets or sheaths. This prevents the claws becoming worn and blunt. When a cat wants to extend or unsheath its claws, foot and toe muscles pull the claws out and down, ready for action. Claws are used for grabbing prey, gripping when climbing, scratching in defence and grooming.

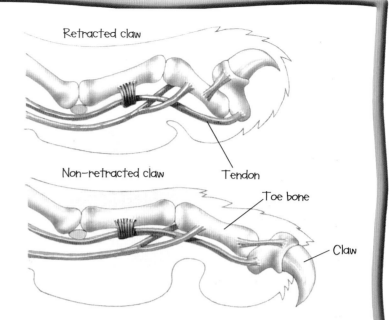

▲ Normally the claws are pulled up or retracted. To extend them, muscles in the legs pull rope–like tendons to move the toe bones and tilt the claw down.

30

Cats often leap, run and climb up trees or along ledges, walls, fences and branches – yet their amazing balance means they hardly ever fall. The tail is very important at these times. The cat can swish or bend its tail to help its balance when walking along a narrow ledge or branch.

▼ A cat's skeleton has most of the bones that we have. The main extra ones are in the tail.

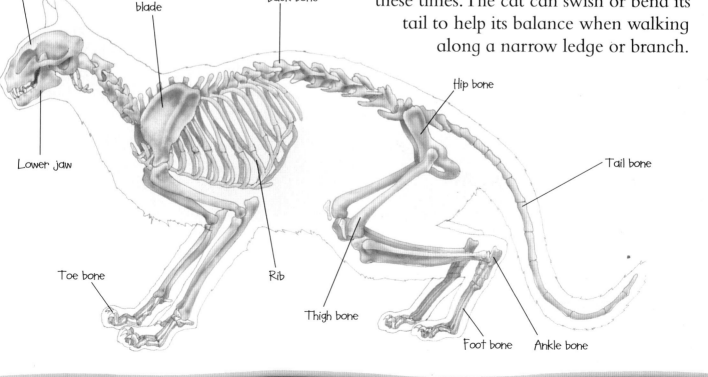

Skull

Shoulder blade

Back bone

Lower jaw

Hip bone

Tail bone

Toe bone

Rib

Thigh bone

Foot bone

Ankle bone

19

Feeling sensitive

Pupil
closed

▲ In bright daylight the cat's pupil narrows to a slit, allowing less light in.

Pupil
open

▲ In darkness the pupil widens to let in as much light as possible, and may become a circle.

Nictitating
membrane

◀ A cat has a 'third eyelid' called the haw or nictitating membrane, on the inner side of its eye. This can move partly across to protect the eyeball.

31 Cats have better hearing than us – especially for high-pitched noises such as mouse squeaks. Also, a cat can twitch and move its ears to find out which direction a sound is coming from. It does not have to turn its whole head, as we have to.

32 A cat has large eyes to see well in the dark. At the front of the eye is a black area called the pupil. If it is nightime, the pupil opens wide to let in as much light as possible. In daytime the pupil narrows to a slit, to stop too much light damaging the eye. Also, there is a mirror-like layer at the back of the eye called the tapetum. This bounces or reflects light within the eye, which helps the cat to see better in darkness.

THE CAT'S WHISKERS

You will need:
drinking straws sticky-tape
1. Fasten some drinking straws to the edges of your sabre-toothed cat mask (page 9) with sticky-tape.
2. Put the mask on and walk around. Can you feel when your whiskers touch something, even with your eyes closed?

33 **A cat's sense of smell is better than ours, but not as good as a dog's.** Cats sniff food and drink to check they are safe. They also smell the scents of their owners, other people, other cats, and any animals nearby. Familiar scents mean a cat is happy and relaxed. Strange scents make it nervous.

34 **Cats often rub their faces against their owners, as well as furniture and other objects around their home.** The cat is spreading its own scent substances from parts called glands around its face and cheeks. This marks out the cat's home area or territory and warns strange cats to stay away.

35 **A cat's tongue not only tastes food and drink, it's also used for cleaning and grooming.** The tongue has a very rough upper surface, like a file or rasp. The cat uses this to scrape meat off bones, drink, and clean its own fur and skin. When a cat drinks, its tongue becomes spoon-shaped to scoop up the liquid. This is called lapping. The tongue can also be pushed out a long way so that the cat can lick around its mouth, whiskers and nose.

36 **The extra-long hairs on the sides of a cat's nose are its whiskers.** The skin at their bases detect any movements of the whiskers. This helps the cat to 'feel its way' in the dark.

▶ A cat rubs scent from its cheeks onto familiar objects – from a chair to its owner. This is the cat's way of saying: 'I live here and own these things – so other cats should keep clear!'

Do cats have nine lives?

37 There is an old saying that 'a cat has nine lives' – but of course this is not really true. It actually means that cats often seem to survive dangers and hazards that other animals can't. This is because of a cat's keen senses, quick reactions, strong muscles and great balance.

▲ Cats may seem to get stuck up trees, especially when young and not experienced in climbing. However, if left alone, and not frightened by noisy people crowding around below it, the cat can often work out how to climb down safely.

38 Another old saying is 'curiosity killed the cat'. This has some truth. Cats are naturally curious. They want to find out what is around corners and above or below things. This probably comes from their wild behaviour long ago, when looking for food. Cats sometimes squeeze into narrow spaces, but after a time they usually get themselves out of these tight spots.

39 A cat's excellent balance and fast reactions mean that it can fall from high places yet usually lands unhurt. The cat twists its body around as it falls. Then it straightens its legs to point downwards, and immediately gets ready to bend its legs as it touches down on all four feet, to cushion the shock of landing.

40 A cat is quick to defend itself against enemies. Its hair stands on end, so the cat looks twice as big. It also snarls and hisses and bares its teeth, showing off these sharp weapons. This serves as a warning to the enemy to keep away or risk being harmed. It is best not to get too close to a cat that is behaving like this, as it may strike out in fear and self-defence.

▼ A frightened cat crouches with ears flattened and teeth bared, ready to defend itself.

I DON'T BELIEVE IT!
Occasionally, cats have been accidentally locked in their houses by owners going on holiday. Some cats have lived without food for more than two weeks, surviving only on water in drops of condensation on glass windows.

▼ Stray cats can make litter problems worse by tearing open waste bags and dragging old meat from bins.

41 There are various names for pet cats who have no human owners or safe homes, and so 'live wild'. These names include feral, stray and alley cats. They sometimes attack and harm pet cats and can also cause a nuisance and health hazard by spreading pests such as fleas and raiding dustbins and rubbish heaps for leftover food.

Cat habits

42 **Cats are usually very clean animals and spend a couple of hours each day grooming or 'washing' themselves.** The cat bends and twists to lick almost every part of its body with its rough tongue. This gets rid of dirt, old skin, loose fur and tiny pests. The cat may also lick its paw, rub this on a body part to clean it, then lick its paw again. And it may run its claws through its fur to get rid of dirt.

43 **Most cats like being brushed by their owners.** This is especially important for long-haired cats, which cannot keep their thick fur clean by themselves. Getting a cat used to being brushed takes time and patience. Start with a few gentle strokes of the brush, stay calm, make no sudden moves, and stroke and fuss the cat afterwards. Over many days the cat will get used to being brushed and begin to enjoy it.

▲ When washing itself, a cat pays special attention to its paws. Bits of dirt, twigs or small stones may get stuck between its toes. The cat must carefully remove these and also lick clean any small nicks or cuts.

Cats spend up to one-third of their waking time cleaning and grooming themselves.

◄ Long-haired cat breeds, like this American Curl, should have regular grooming sessions from their owners. Otherwise tangles, dirt and pests start to collect in its long, thick fur.

I DON'T BELIEVE IT!

Cats sometimes eat grass! This is natural. Grass gives cats extra nutrients. Plants also help a cat to cough up stuck food or furballs.

44 **Cats often seem to be sick – but they are really coughing up, or regurgitating, furballs or hairballs.** These are lumps of fur that the cat swallows while grooming, and that mat together as a slimy mass in its stomach. Coughing up furballs is healthy. Otherwise the furball might block the cat's intestines and cause real sickness.

45 **Cats like to scratch – in fact, they need to.** The cat usually stretches out its front legs and pulls with its claws at something rough and hard, like wood. This is not so much to keep its claws sharp, but to stretch and exercise its muscles and joints. For cats kept indoors, a purpose-made scratching post helps to save the curtains!

▲ A scratching post can be purpose-made, or simply be an old piece of wood.

25

Cat comforts

46 **Most cats like being stroked.** But, like picking up a cat, you should start by doing this carefully and calmly, so the cat comes to trust you. Sudden moves or noises, or forcing a cat to be stroked, only make it more wary and nervous. Along the back, the cheek and behind the ears are good places. This is where cats 'stroke' us by rubbing themselves against our legs. Always stroke a cat in the same direction that its fur lies in.

▼ Let a cat come to you, rather than rushing after it. Stroke it gently and calmly. This way the cat will gain confidence and soon come to enjoy it.

47 **A cat's miaow can mean many different things.** A loud, high-pitched miaow may mean, 'I'm hungry!' A quieter, short miaow like a squeaky door, may be a welcoming sign, like saying 'Hello friend!' The sounds a cat makes come from its voice-box or larynx which, like our own voice-box, is in the neck. Some cat breeds miaow more than others. Siamese cats are well-known for being noisy.

48

Cats usually purr when they are happy, relaxed and content. The purr comes, not from the cat's voice-box, but from its breathing muscles deep in its chest. The rattling or vibrating sound can also be felt if you touch a loudly purring cat!

▲ A happy purring cat may narrow its eyes and stretch its front paws forwards one after the other as if 'paddling'.

CAN YOU PURR?

Try various ways to copy a cat's purring sound. For example, let your loose tongue rattle against the roof of your mouth as you breathe out.

49

Cats are famous for their cat-naps – short periods of snoozing and dozing. The cat is usually quite alert when napping, and will leap up at the slightest worry. In general, cats prefer warm, quiet places for napping and sleeping. This is why they often sleep behind chairs or in corners. They also like places that smell right – often of their owners. This is why cats may curl up on their owner's clothes, chairs or beds. Cats like to fall asleep in the sunshine too, seeking out sunny spots to keep warm.

▶ This Abyssinian cat has found a sunny spot on a draining board. Cats don't find the most practical places to fall asleep, but that's all part of their character.

Friend or foe?

50 Cats have moods, like us, and it helps if we recognize these. A tiny movement, faint sound or smell that we cannot detect, can worry a cat. It may suddenly become alert and ready for action. A scared cat crouches low, flattens its ears, opens its mouth, hisses, bristles its fur and swishes its tail low. Then it's best to leave the cat alone, so it can run off or hide if it wishes.

◄ Cats wail, screech and cry to tell other cats of their presence, saying 'This area is not free – I live here'.

51 Cats may seem to bring home 'presents' of small creatures such as half–dead mice and wounded birds. Often the cat does not kill its victim, but chases, pounces and 'plays' with it. This may seem cruel to us, but the cat is simply following its natural behaviour and instincts. It is practising its hunting skills in familiar surroundings.

◄ Kittens play with almost anything that moves, such as falling leaves, to rehearse their hunting actions.

52 Cats often 'caterwaul', making loud wails and screeches – especially at night. Usually they are warning other cats away from their territory. A cat's territory is its home area, where it likes to roam, rest and hunt without fear of interference by other cats. Territories vary greatly in size. They may be just a room in the owner's house, or the whole house, the garden too, or even part of a street, park or wood.

▶ A young cat and dog who grow up in the same place often become excellent friends – perhaps even more so than two young cats.

53 **A cat and dog can be best friends, especially if brought up together as kitten and puppy.** But if a cat and dog are strangers, they are often less friendly. The cat may bare its claws, fluff its fur, and get ready to hiss in self-defence. But like any animal, it usually prefers to avoid danger and escape.

54 **Some cats, especially toms (males), spray urine around their territory – and this may include the house!** The urine has scents that other cats detect, and which warn these cats to stay away. A vet's advice may be needed for a troublesome tom who sprays urine in the house.

I DON'T BELIEVE IT!

Cat flaps can have computers! One design of cat flap only opens when a computer chip comes near – and the chip is on a safe elastic collar around the cat's neck.

29

Keeping healthy

55 Cats sometimes fall ill, but we can prevent some serious illnesses by giving them injections called vaccinations. The two main injections protect against feline influenza or 'cat flu', and feline infectious enteritis, an infection by virus germs. The vet advises when to give these, usually in kittens from the age of eight weeks.

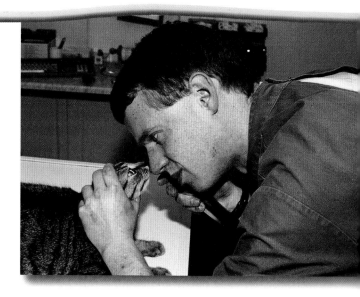

▲ Vets are experts at handling animals, and soon put a worried cat at ease so it can be checked and examined.

56 Cats can show various signs of illness. These may include coughs, sneezes, fluids such as pus or discharge from the eyes, nose or ears, being sick or vomiting, diarrhoea, trembling and fur loss.

57 Cat owners should stay alert for signs of illness in their pets. Sometimes these are obvious, such as a runny nose. Other signs are difficult to pinpoint, such as loss of appetite or being 'off food', and a dull coat rather than shiny fur.

58 Apart from an occasional cough or sneeze, if a cat seems ill then it's best to contact a vet by phone and describe the signs. The vet can advise on home treatment or whether to take the cat to the veterinary centre for a proper examination.

◄ A cat-carrier (cat-cage or cat-conveyor) keeps the cat safe on journeys such as to the vet. Trying to hold a nervous, ill cat in your arms is far too risky.

A cat's eyes compared to its whole head
are six times bigger than your eyes
compared to your whole head.

59

A cat that scratches lots, often quite suddenly, may have tiny pests such as fleas, lice, mites and ticks. They can sometimes be seen crawling in the fur or their droppings may look like dark dust. Also, they can spread and bite us! Most kinds of pests can be killed with special powders, shampoos or sprays. Fleas can be kept away with a cat flea collar.

60

A cat that seems to eat lots but stay thin and 'off colour' may have worms. These include long, ribbon-like tapeworms and smaller, squirmy roundworms. Sometimes the worms or their eggs are seen in the cat's droppings. Pills or injections can kill these worms.

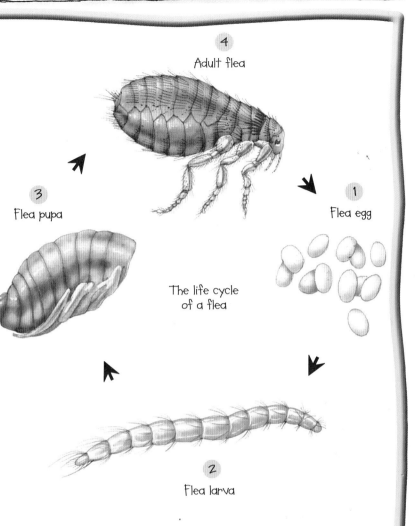

4
Adult flea

3
Flea pupa

1
Flea egg

The life cycle of a flea

2
Flea larva

▲ Cat fleas are dark brown and not much larger than a pin-head. The adult flea lays tiny eggs which hatch into worm-like larvae or grubs. These grow hard casings and become pupae, then the adult flea breaks out of the case.

QUIZ

Which of these signs would need a vet's attention?
A. Coughing and fast, shallow breathing that goes on for hours
B. Short single cough
C. Drinking lots of water or other liquid whenever possible
D. Small single sneeze
E. Lots of sneezing plus a runny nose and eyes

Answers:
B and D are not too worrying provided they are one-offs. The other signs could mean a serious illness. Contact the vet without delay.

61

A tiny worm called toxocara can spread from cats, usually from their droppings, to people and occasionally cause blindness. This is why it's important to wash your hands after handling cats and their equipment, especially litter trays.

Starting a family

62 Pet cats breed like most other animals. A male (tom), and a female (queen) mate. The female becomes pregnant with developing babies – kittens. This can happen only at certain times of the year. The female is ready to mate around March to April, then through midsummer in June, and around September. Usually the female does not mate until she is 7 to 12 months old, and a male before 10 to 13 months of age.

I DON'T BELIEVE IT!
Most mother cats have about four to six kittens in a litter. But sometimes there can be as many as 12.

63 After mating, a mother cat is pregnant (which is known as her gestation period) for an average of **65 days.** But this varies from 60 to 70 days, depending on the breed of cat, the mother's age and other features.

64 An expectant mother cat gains one to two kilograms in weight and her tummy grows in size. Near the birth she searches for a nest or den where she can have her kittens in peace and quiet. This can be almost anywhere she feels comfortable and safe – from the corner of a shed, a clump of grass at the end of the garden, or behind the sofa. Most owners try to provide a kittening box or basket and hope the mother will give birth there.

65 Usually a mother cat gives birth to all her kittens within a day. At first she pants and purrs. Then the kittens arrive one by one, along with the bag-like membranes they grew within, inside the womb. The mother bites through the umbilical cord, which joins the kitten's tummy. This carried nourishment to the kitten when it was in the womb. Then she licks and cleans each kitten in turn, and finally feeds them before resting.

◀ Giving birth to a litter of hungry, squeaking new kittens is hard work, and may take all day and night. When they have all been born, the mother allows her kittens to suckle her milk while she rests.

New kittens

66 New baby kittens are almost helpless. Their ears are folded back and their eyes are closed, so they cannot hear or see. They cannot walk or even crawl. These bundles of fluff depend fully on their mother, who stays with them and keeps them safe in their nest or den. The mother licks and cleans them often, and their eyes start to open after about a week.

◄ Newborn kittens are tiny, weak and unable to see or hear properly.

67 One of the few things a new kitten can do is suckle – feed on milk from its mother. Each kitten in the litter has its own teat (nipple) on the mother's underside, which it sucks to obtain the milk. If a kitten is hungry, it makes small squeaking noises to let its mother know.

▼ At three weeks kittens look around, listen, and are able to crawl or shuffle.

▲ Once kittens are one week old their eyes are just opening and their legs can stretch and scrabble.

68 Every few days, the mother cat may move her kittens to a new nest or den. She picks up each one in her mouth by the loose skin on the back of its neck (the scruff) and carries it quietly to the new nest. This often happens if the mother is disturbed or feels the existing nest is unsafe.

◄ When they are four weeks old kittens are able to walk and start to run and play.

QUIZ

How old are kittens when the following stages of kitten growth usually happen?
1. Eyes start to open
2. Begins to crawl or shuffle
3. Starts to walk
4. Starts to eat solid foods
5. Stops taking mother's milk

Answers:
1. 1 week 2. Three weeks
3. Four weeks 4. Four weeks
5. Eight weeks

69 **The mother cat and kittens soon come to know each other in many ways.** As they lie near each other, their body scents spread between them, so they can all recognize each other by smell. The mother also knows her kittens by sight and sound as they mew for milk.

70 **A mother cat's milk gives her kittens all the nourishment they need for the first three or four weeks after birth.** Then the kittens start to eat other foods as well, called solids. By about eight weeks old, the kittens usually stop suckling. This changeover from milk to normal foods is called weaning.

◄ Once a kitten is eight weeks old it is active, playful, entertaining and just about ready to continue life without its mother.

Growing up

71 From about four weeks of age, kittens can run and jump – and then they start to play! They race about, spring up and leap down, climb almost anything, and sometimes bump into things or fall over.

▼ A mother cat 'rescues' lost kittens and carries them back to safety. She gently holds the youngster by the loose skin at the back of the neck, known as the 'scruff'.

72 By six or seven weeks old, the kittens start to 'play– hunt'. They chase each other's twitching tails, and pounce on small objects such as fluffy balls or toy mice. They use their teeth and claws to scratch and grab.

73 After about a month, the kittens are strong enough to 'go walkabout' with their mother. They follow her as they wander about, sniffing and pawing at things. They watch her tail as a guide to where she is.

74 If a kitten gets lost or separated, it usually makes a squeaky mewing noise. The mother cat miaows back, or comes to find the lost kitten and carry it back to the nest. As the kitten gains in confidence and begins to explore, the mother cat will need to 'rescue' it less.

75 **Most kittens are ready to leave their mother and be taken to a new owner by eight weeks of age.** If they stay with the mother, they may leave by themselves after about six months.

76 **Some people do not want their young cat to have kittens.** So they take it to the vet for a small operation, which removes the body parts that are used for breeding. This is called spaying for female cats and can be done after 15 weeks of age. It is known as neutering for male cats and can take place after 35 weeks.

77 **Kittens can get so excited as they play that they use their tiny sharp teeth and claws on almost anything — including us.** If a kitten feels in danger it will hiss, spit and scratch. So an adult should always be around when young children play with a kitten, and warn the children not to put the kitten near their faces.

▼ Kittens who are litter-mates (sisters and brothers) usually stay good friends. They play together well, even though their 'games' may become rough as they get older.

Different breeds

78 All pet or domestic cats belong to one kind, or species. Within this species there are many different types (breeds) of pet cats. They vary in size, body build, coat colour and pattern, fur length, eye colour and other features. Some breeds weigh an average of less than 2.5 kilograms, while others are twice as heavy.

▲ The Manx breed with no tail at all is called a 'rumpy' Manx. If it has just a tiny short stump for a tail it is known as a 'stumpy' Manx.

79 The many breeds of cats have been decided by people. Cats with certain features, such as a new fur colour or pattern are selected to mate and have kittens. Then people choose which of the kittens should breed, and so on. This is called selective breeding. Over many years it has produced more than 100 cat breeds.

▲ The tabby is the 'original' colour for a pet cat. If all pet cats were allowed to breed with each other for several years, and not be selected by breeders, then most would end up as tabbies.

80 One of the most common cat coat colours is a mix of black, brown and tawny swirls, stripes and spots. This is called the tabby or 'moggie'. The first domestic cats, thousands of years ago, were probably a similar colour to this.

A tortoiseshell cat (with ginger, black and cream fur) is almost certain to be female.

81 One of the most famous cat breeds is the Siamese. It is long and slim, with small paws and intense blue eyes. About 500 years ago these cats were kept by the kings of Siam, the region now known as Thailand. Siamese cats tend to be very affectionate to their owners. They can also be quite noisy, with a loud miaow.

◀ A Siamese cat has slim, elegant body proportions.

COLOUR YOUR OWN CAT

You will need:
large sheets of card   coloured pens
crayons or paints.

You can make a new breed of cat in a few minutes – but only on paper. Draw a cat outline. Colour the fur with your favourite shades and patterns. Choose an eye colour too, like blue, green or yellow. What will you name your new breed of cat?

82 The British Blue is the best-known of the breeds called British Shorthairs. In fact its 'short hair' is quite long and thick, with a grey-blue sheen. It also has striking orange or copper-coloured eyes, small ears and short legs. This breed was one of the first to be displayed when cat shows started over a hundred years ago.

▶ The British Blue's fur is dense, meaning the hairs grow very close together.

83 The Persian breeds of cat are also known as Longhairs. Their fur is long and thick, and they need help from their owners with their grooming. There are many colours of Persians, from pure white to jet black, and also tabby and tortoiseshell breeds. Their name comes from the region once known as Persia (now Iran) in west Asia. The earliest Persian breeds of cats arrived in Europe during the late 1500s.

Strange breeds

84 The Scottish Folds breed began in 1961 with 'Susie', a white kitten who lived on a farm near Coupar Angus in Tayside, Scotland. Her unusual ears were bent forwards and down. A shepherd named William Ross noticed Susie. He bred her with a local male cat. Two of Susie's kittens had folded ears too, and so this new breed began.

▶ It takes a while for a new breed like the Scottish Folds to become established, and to be accepted by the organizations who run cat shows and the official lists of breeds or pedigrees.

▼ The tail of the Japanese Bobtail has hairs growing out all around, giving a fluffy effect like a rabbit's tail.

85 The Japanese Bobtail breed is named after its very short or 'bobbed' tail. Most of these cats have a tortoiseshell-and-white colour pattern known in Japan as Mi-Ke. Other colours include black-and-white and red (brown)-and-white. Often when this cat sits upright, it raises one of its front feet as though about to 'shake paws' – a gesture which Japanese people say means good luck. The Japanese Bobtail has a sturdy body, long back legs, large ears and big eyes. Its tail measures around 10 centimetres and is usually curled in, close to the body.

86
The Maine Coon was one of the first cat breeds from North America. It is large and strong, with a thick shaggy coat that is usually brown and black, and a white chest and paws. It is named after the northeast US state of Maine, where it probably began, and it has similar colouring and hunting methods as the raccoon. Maine Coons probably started as farm cats. They still search out strange places to sleep, like on rooftops or under floorboards.

◀ The Maine Coon can make a strange, quiet miaowing sound, similar to a bird chirping.

87
The Sphynx breed is perhaps the most unusual pet cat – it has no fur. It started in Canada in 1966 when one kitten in a litter was born without fur. The Sphynx is friendly and quiet, but it is not keen on being held or cuddled too much. It has large ears and small paws. The only hairs are short, dark, fine 'down' on its face, ears, feet and tail tip. It is an ideal cat for people that are allergic to animal fur.

▲ Most pet cats, if they lost their fur, would have a similar shape to the Sphynx breed.

I DON'T BELIEVE IT!
Longhaired cats that become homeless have particular trouble surviving in the wild, because their fur gets dirty, tangled, wet and full of pests.

Showtime!

88 There are many official clubs and organizations for breeding cats and showing them in competitions, displays and exhibitions. They include the British Governing Council of the Cat Fancy (GCCF), the Cat Fanciers' Association (CFA) of America, and others in almost every country. People who run these groups include cat breeders, cat exhibitors and cat fanciers (cat fans).

▲ The Supreme Cat Show is licensed by the GCCF. It is held each year in Birmingham. There is also a section for non-pedigree cats.

▼ London's Crystal Palace was the site of the first major cat show. Today, shows held in huge exhibition halls and conference centres attract thousands of cats and owners.

89 The first proper cat show was organized by Harrison Weir in London in 1871. It was held at the Crystal Palace and included 25 different competitions or classes for Persians, British Shorthairs and other breeds. Soon after, cat shows were held in the New England region of northeast North America, mainly for the Maine Coon breed.

90 Today there are countless cat shows around the world.
They vary from huge international gatherings, where cats and owners fly in from many countries, to local shows in a town or village, where children can show off their family pets.

Head shape

Ear shape and size

Eye colour, size and spacing

Whisker length and number

Leg length and proportions – slim or sturdy

Paw size and shape – round or oval

Tail length and fluffiness

Fur colour and pattern

Coat length and density (thickness)

▲ Cats, such as this Persian, are judged on every feature of their head, body, legs, tail and coat, as well as their behaviour and temperament – from relaxed and friendly, to nervous, shy or scared.

91 The main show in Britain is the GCCF Supreme Cat Show.
This began in 1976 and only cats that have won at other championship shows can enter. It takes place every November at the National Exhibition Centre, Birmingham. The International Cat Association, TICA, organizes shows in North America, Europe and many other regions, from Brazil and Argentina to Korea and Japan.

MAKE YOUR CAT A CHAMPION!

You will need:
large sheets of card   safe scissors
coloured pens or crayons.

Pretend your cat has won top prize at an important show. Real champions receive a rosette, an official certificate, and perhaps a cup. You can make these from cut-out paper or card, and colour them, perhaps on a computer.

Cat tales

92 **In Japan, models and statues of cats are seen as lucky charms.** A Japanese legend tells of a priest who lived in a temple with his cat. A man travelling past the temple saw the cat raise its paw and beckon him to enter. As he did, a bolt of lightning hit the spot where he had been standing. He was very grateful to the cat for saving his life. Statues of beckoning cats are found all over Japan and are believed to bring good luck.

▲ 'Come to me and you will have good fortune' says the pose of the Japanese lucky-charm cat statue.

93 **Black cats are mysterious creatures that seem to come and go unseen among the shadows of the night.** They became famous as the companions of witches and wizards, and some people believed they could cast their own spells. There are even tales of cats that were 'familiars' – a type of spirit in animal form.

◀ Tales of witchcraft and magic often feature a black cat.

The Bombay breed of cat is jet black and incredibly friendly – it rarely stops purring and worries if it is left alone.

94 Some people believe black cats are lucky, while others say that they bring very bad luck! This is especially true if a black cat crosses your path – walks or runs across in front of you. However, there is no scientific proof for any of these beliefs.

▲ Black cats behave in much the same way as other cats – taking every chance to relax!

MAKE A SPOOKY HAT – AND A SPOOKY CAT

You will need:
black card   safe scissors
a stapler   elastic
1. Carefully cut out two pointed hat shapes.
2. Staple them around the edges, then push them open in the middle to make a hat.
3. Cut out a black card cat that you can hold and talk to while making spells.
4. Paint its eyes red or green.
5. A black cloak might help to complete your spooky outfit!

95 In medieval times in Europe, cats were hated, hunted and even killed by some people of the Christian religion. This is perhaps because they were linked to witchcraft and to other rival religions. For example, the goddess Freyja of Norse legend had a chariot drawn by cats.

▶ Freyja's chariot was pulled by two large, fierce wildcats.

96 There are many superstitions linked to cat behaviour. A cat that washes its ears is said to foretell rain and bad weather. A cat that twitches its feet while asleep is said to be dreaming of its afterlife in heaven. If you stare at a cat and blink your eyes slowly, the cat may blink back, which is said to be a sign of friendship.

Famous cats

97 Many cats feature as characters in novels, fairytales and nursery rhymes. Have you heard the stories about clever, cunning Puss-in-Boots, by Charles Perrault? When you were young you may have read the 'nonsense poem' by Edward Lear about the owl and the pussycat, who went to sea in a beautiful pea-green boat. And which nursery rhyme features a cat and a fiddle?

▲ Puss-in-Boots is a very clever cat. He gives gifts to the king so that his owner, a poor miller's son, can marry the king's daughter, a beautiful princess.

▼ In their boat the owl and the pussycat took some honey and plenty of money, wrapped up in... what?

98 Cats have been heroes in many cartoons and animations. In fact, one of the very first cartoon stories in newspapers and magazines was *Krazy Kat*, which started in 1913. Today we have the lazy ginger cat Garfield in the daily newspaper, and the comic-book cartoon superhero Catwoman. There is also Sylvester the cat who famously chases Tweety Pie in the animated cartoon.

99 There are many famous cats in books and stories. *The Cat in the Hat* books are known around the world. Bouncing Tigger is a famous friend of the bear Winnie the Pooh. More serious is Mowgli's friend Bagheera the black panther in *The Jungle Book*. The famous musical show *Cats* is based on the book *Old Possum's Book of Practical Cats* by T S Eliot. Perhaps strangest is the wide-smiling Cheshire Cat in *Alice's Adventures in Wonderland*. It could slowly disappear until all that was left was its grin. Alice said that she'd often seen a cat without a grin, but never a grin without a cat.

▼ Bagheera was the boy Mowgli's friend in *The Jungle Book*, written by Rudyard Kipling in 1894. It was made into an animated movie with award-winning songs in 1967.

100 There are many famous cats on television and in the movies, who have also been made into toys and games. Little children love to read about Bagpuss, and Postman Pat's black-and-white cat Jess. Then there's the Disney movie *The Aristocats*, the exciting TV series *Thundercats*… can you think of any more famous film-star cats?

◄ Top Cat is a lovable character from the cartoon show of the same name. It was first screened in 1961.

47

Index